ALAND A LAND

-

By JEANNIE CARLSON

All poetry contained in this work is the original work of the author.

Published by St. Petersburg Press
St. Petersburg, FL
www.stpetersburgpress.com

Design and composition by St. Petersburg Press and Isa Crosta
Cover design by Isa Crosta
Cover photo by Timothy R. Burns

Quotes from Carl M. Carlson (pages 41, 153, 181, 197, 219, 247, 255, and
261) are reprinted by permission from *Pastime - A Swede in America Looks
Back: The Life Journal of Carl M. Carlson* translated by Richard E. Gingrich,
copyright 1992.

Print ISBN: 978-1-964239-35-4
Ebook ISBN: 978-1-964239-36-1

First Edition

ALAND A LAND

By JEANNIE CARLSON

ACKNOWLEDGEMENTS

First I need to recognize my father's cousin, Richard E. Gingrich (1929-2022) who edited our ancestor's journal, *Pastime: A Swede in America Looks Back* by Carl M. Carlson; which inspired my search for our family's history in the Al- and Islands.

Thanks to my uncle, The Rev. Robert W. Carlson (1929-2022) who planned our American family trip (16 of us at the time) to Scandinavia which took place in 2007. The highlight of the trip was the Aland Islands where we met our Swedish cousins.

Thanks to Dr. Linda Quennec, friend, colleague, and award-winning author of the novel, *Fishing for Birds*, for her input.

Thanks to Jake Zarnowski, a multimedia wiz and good friend, for helping me create the technical aspects of the digital artwork included in my investigative poetics project of the Aland Islands.

Thanks to Susan Thornton of the Tampa Chapter of the National League of American Pen Women for providing the map in 2014 of the Aland Islands.

Thanks to everyone on the St. Petersburg Press team who helped make this book a reality. Special thanks go to Amy Cianci, my favorite Engagement Director for her skill and dedication that contributed to the success of this project, our second book together.

Thanks to my family, those here in America and those in Scandinavia; those from the past and the present as well as those yet to come. Loving all of you is a timeless blessing. May this book be a link to our ancestry, and to one other.

Thanks to my husband, Tim Burns, and to my son, Phil Carlson. The contribution of their photos, and, most importantly, their encouragement helped make this project a reality.

Thanks to my cousins, Arthur, Paul and Eddie for sharing ancestral photos for this project.

Soli Deo Gloria

In memory of my uncle, The Rev. Dr. Robert W. Carlson, and my father's cousin, Richard E. Gingrich, both grandsons of Carl M. Carlson.

Contents

Map of the Aland Islands courtesy of Susan Thornton,
NLAPW, 2014

Autonomous state of
Åland

Bothnian Sea

Finnish
mainland

Brändö

Geta   Saltvik

Kumlinge

*Archipelago
Sea*

Vårdö

Finström   Sund

Hammarland

Eckerö   Jomala

Lumparland

*Sea of
Åland*

Mariehamn

Sottunga

Lemland   Föglö   Kökar

Swedish
mainland

Baltic Sea

SWEDEN   FINLAND

▪ ▪ ▪	National boundary
- - -	Regional boundary
·········	Boudary of municipality
Sund	Name of municipality

Digital Art by Jeannie Carlson, 2023
"Aland" in ancient runic on granite

ALAND IN RUNIC

ᚠᛁᚠᛏᛗ

ALAND, A LAND

Visualize a strand of Aland DNA

LEGEND

Tall
Tall stories
Tall sailors
Tall Vikings
Tall Alanders
Tall and taller

~

Carl Mauritz Carlson circa 1890s

1000 AD

Hlodver the Tall from Saltvik
Helmsman on the *Ormen Lange*
Taller than tall and longer than long
Titanic bootlegging snake
Sailed to Poland
Handpicked by Viking King Olav Tryggvason
Questing Queen Tyra's inheritance
Ambushed in naval battle at Svolder
Fought like an Alander beside his king
Died an Alander
An island on water

~

Arthur M. Carlson, photoengraver, NYC circa 1930s

1885 AD

Carl Mauritz Carlson from Eckero
Son of Carl Magnus Danielson and Anna Katrina Johnson
Forged out of Storby's harbor like a bowl, *Charingsund*
Six foot six, a mythic echo
Holding true to the Baltic Sea at sixteen
Matrosas, able seamen in Swedish
Threw the anchor out at the bow
And tied the stern to the shore
Eckero to Alholmana, Sweden
Sunsval, Sweden to Antwerp, Belgium
Gotland and Olamand on the starboard side
Helsingfors on the Danish side and Helsingborg on the Swedish side
Dunkirk, France to Arindel, Norway
Copenhagen to Stockholm
Pelo, Germany to New York Harbor
A fair wind blew hard half a topsail
Escaping the Czar's impressments

~

Carlson family, Brooklyn, NY pre-WWI
Standing from left: sons Arthur and Carl
Seated from left: Mathilda and Carl, Sr., parents,
with daughter Helen

1942 AD

Lloyd Arthur Carlson
Grandson of Carl
Son of Arthur
Offspring of Aland
Seed of the sea at eighteen
Six foot even or a little more
Launched into a second world war
Cruiser light *USS Miami*

Poured into tumult
Battle medals mounting
ASIATIC-PACIFIC MEDAL WITH SIX STARS
VICTORY MEDAL
AMERICAN AREA MEDAL
PHILLIPPINE LIBERATION MEDAL WITH TWO
STARS

Halsey's Third Fleet
Halsey's Typhoon
Halsey's great boon

Seaman see man

~

Lloyd Arthur Carlson, sailor WWII, circa 1942

TALE

All
All over six feet
All six feet under
All sailing seas
All seeing sails
All and all over

~

USS Miami CL-89

Commissioned 1943 – Decommissioned 1947

Stricken 1961 – Sold for Scrap 1962

U.S.S MIAMI

~

"If you are looking for a brave seaman, you have to go to a Fisherman's village, for he is without fear on the water."

Carl Mauritz Carlson

1869-1941

FREYJA'S BONES

Granite earth presiding over *Sessrumnir* filled with half a
heaven of battlefield warriors fallen into her arms
where
       plants
              places
                     art
                         women

bear her name
bare her claim
around their necks
like *Brisingamen's* flaming ornament
cloaked in falcon feathers
jockeying chariots driven by a pair of felines
frothing at the mouth
blue and breathless
pursued by vigorous *jotnar* giants jostling
intending her possession but
burnt and reborn
her namesakes own the archipelago
alchemists all
bought with her tears of red gold

(Norse: goddess of love & fertility)

(Norse: "seat-roomer," Freyja's hall or ship in Folkvangr's afterlife)

(Norse:"flaming/glowing" Freyja's magic necklace)

(Norse: giants from a race of giants living among rocks)

Danielson Hus

Sometime in the 1970s my uncle travelled to Aland to see the homestead where our ancestors lived in Eckero for four hundred years. In the village everyone knew the Danielson house so it was easy to find. He knocked on the door of the house built of many sized pine logs lined with boards painted red outside. He was not expected. Welcomed inside, he was served coffee and Aland's Pankakken, a cardamom farina pudding dessert and given the recipe. Thirty years later our Aland cousins greeted us, the next two generations at the docks of Mariehamn. The house had been demolished six weeks before.

~

Danielson House, Eckero, Aland

Danielson House Ruins

1970

The Reverend Doctor Robert W. Carlson

Brother of Lloyd

Son of Arthur

Grandson of Carl

Blesses the threshold

Six inches below six feet

  Of Four Hundred Years

      Of Eckero Ancestors

Valkommen

2007

Missionary Carl P. Carlson
Nephew of Robert
Grandson of Lloyd
Great Grandson of Arthur
Great-Great Grandson of Carl
Blesses the Great-Great empty space
Two inches below six feet
    The Great-Great ghost
        Aroma
            of coffee and cardamom
    The Great-Great crimson and pine dismantling
        six weeks before
        there is no after

~

Arthur Carlson with his sons, Robert and Lloyd, early 1930s

ENDURING

Two
Empty
Ladder backs
One up one down
One right one left
Leftovers from a separated set
The last of the dining ensemble
From a century passed
Traveled the Atlantic
Served five generations
A smorgasbord many times over

MOR LORE

Far Far Mor

Euphemia Matilda Mattson
A child of Jomala, "Tilda"
   Of 1871
   Of Wilhelmina Danielsdotter dead when you toddled at 3
Adventuress
   Sailing to New York
   Maiding to Madison Avenue
Married transplanted Alander
   Tall enough yourself
   Taller than enough
Mother
   To an eldest son, then twining boys, one living, one not
   To daughters Helen of Brooklyn and Florence of Heaven
Woman
   Baking chocolate cake for a Sunday orphan
   Speaking only English in a Swedish home
Sister
   Separated from a sibling by an ocean
   Reunited descendants by a century-old wish
Spirit
   Released after 53 years
   Here and there and there

(Swedish: Mother)

(Swedish: Father's Father's Mother)

Euphemia Mathilda Mattson Carlson, 1890s

GOING ALAND POSTAL: 1638-1917

Sixteen thirty-eight
The first letter is sent
The first letter arrives
The post road newly bent
Kastelholm and Eckero
Sweden to Finland across Aland descent

Centuries fold war, slows
the post; war changes host
Russia beleaguerer
The Grand Duchy
Cyrillic is scratched on
Cyrillic is cancelled

Until the *Postiljonen**,
Hundreds drown or freeze
Traversing the Aland Sea
Words that never made it
Along with the small boats and sleds
weighed down by giant mail carriers.

(The postal steamer that transported the mail after 1870)

Digital Art by Jeannie Carlson, 2023
Aland butterfly stamps in the shape of the Swedish flag

ALAND BUTTERFLY STAMP SWEDISH FLAG

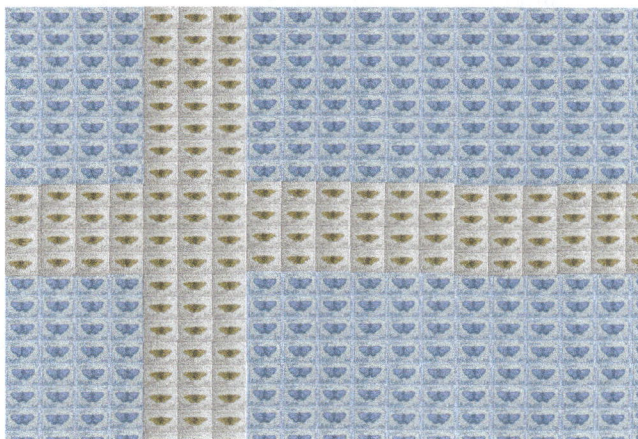

POMMERN

(Sailed the world from 1903-1953. This tall ship was much
like those in which Carl M. Carlson sailed.)

Four-masted barque
towed into Alandic
hands to dock
retire teach bestow devote
exhibit pastime of *gamla* mariners

able bodied seaman
searing soaring siring
Dag Hammarskjold markings

in its original condition

ghost crew stowed in simple forecastle
captain's salon in the ship's stern,
parked in the ice cold paradise
of the archipelago
folded in the arms of Mariehamn
stepping down into the empty cargo hold
smelling of rock salt
and my great grandfather

(Swedish: old)

Pommern, docked in Mariehamn, Aland, 2007

ALL THINGS ALAND *SVENSKA*

Purple violets on the vowel table
*Kroppkakor** cooking *kaffe* percolating
Overring on an audacious A
Abandoned umlauts dangling overhead

Consonant slice servings
Aland pancake farina cardamom
With a lingonberry cream hat
Dressed thickly slow simmer

Double dashes and dairy doses
Wild flowers after Walpurgis
Sleigh rides showering white whinnies
Hand-holding *Lucia* and *Knut*

Phonology of gender tender pitch
Silk diacritics slide into a supple
Copulation joining as they go
Fondling fricatives fondly forward

(Swedish: adjective for "Swedish")

(Swedish: a. bacon & onion stuffed potato dumplings; b. coffee)

(Saint Lucia's Day is Dec. 13 and Saint Knut's Day is Jan. 13, spanning the Christmas/Jul season)

ECKERO

Seven villages sequenced
The length of nearly two thousand Alanders
Lying end to end
And half as wide,
An hour's walk end to end

Storby the most sacred
Reaching back for *Mor*

Eighty generations,
Finland's westernmost flipping finger

Twenty-five miles from Stockholm
A million miles from where it used to be
Entrance to waters of Bothnia
Shallow rocks along the coast
Just beneath the sea

(Swedish: Mother)

Digital Art by Jeannie Carlson, 2023
Aland Statistics in 2007 A.D.

ALAND STATISTICS IN 2007 A.D.

A Mattson Cousin's Summerhouse, 2007

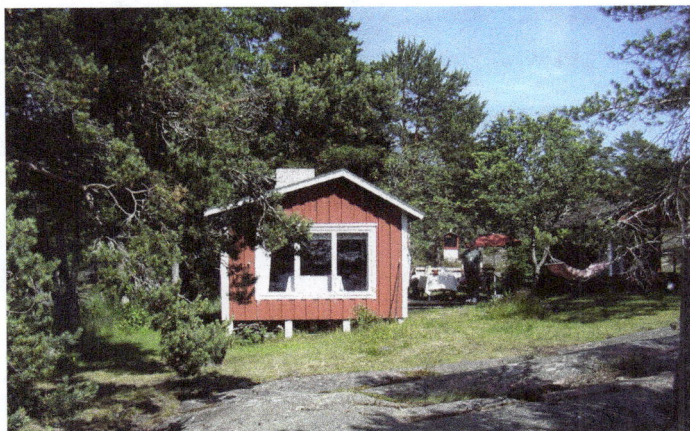

Alandic Lit Days in the Mariehamn Public Library

Alive and dead

   dead and alive

Sally Salminen, Anni Blomqvist, Ulla-Lena Lundberg, Carina Karlsson

Joel Petterson, Valdemar Nyman, Leo Lothman

Women out-write the men

ALAND FRIMARKEN (STAMPS) I: 1984-1987

Aland's
  Flag
  Fishing boats
  Maps
  Shipping
  Midsummer pole
  Forest meadow
  Outer archipelago
  Country scenery
  Orienteering
  Clay hands
  Bronze staff
  Court site
  Artist's colony in Onningeby 100 years
  Common Eider
  Tufted Duck
  Velvet Scoter
  Fire Bridge 100 years
  Farjsund Bridge
  Municipal meeting
  Postal Service 350 years
  Agricultural education 100 years

Walking Street in Mariehamn, Aland, 2007

Digital Art by Jeannie Carlson, 2023
Aland Island municipalities in the oval outline shape
of all the islands together

ALAND ISLAND MUNICIPALITIES

Red Granite Tower, St. Lars Church, 2007

SMORGASBORD 2008
GOD JUL!
Fare

Breads: Wasa Julknacke Wheat Crispbread (Imported),
Limpa Bread

Imported Cheeses: Danish Havarti, Swedish Fontina,
Swedish Herrgard

Entrees: Swedish Sausage with Senap Mustard (Imported)
Kottbullar (Swedish Meatballs)

Seafood: Swedish Gravlaxsas Salmon
Red Lumpfish Kaviar (Imported)
Shrimp Dip

Vegetables & Fruits: Gurka Sallad (Cucumbers in Dill)
Lingonberries (Imported Swedish Wildberries)
Skvade Aptit Rodbetor (Imported Swedish Sliced Beets)

Desserts: Swedish Dala Horse Cake, Christmas Tree Cakes,
Pepparkakkor (Imported Swedish Gingersnap Cookies)

Beverages: Glogg (spiced juices – with & without Claret wine)
Lingonberry Iced Tea
Gevalia Royal Vinter Kaffe (Imported Swedish Decaf Coffee)

SKOL!

From Tim & Jeannie
St. Petersburg
Christmas Day: 1 p.m. - 6 p.m.

~

ALAND FRIMARKEN (STAMPS) II: 1988-1991

Aland's

    Tall ships

    Church of Jomala

    Mariehamn Town Hall

    Elder-flower orchid

    Lady's slipper

    Educational system 350 years

    Church of Finstrom

    Baltic herring

    Pike

    Flounder

    Tufted rug

    Fresco

    Church of Lumparland

    Hedgehog

    Squirrel

    Roe deer

    Aland Island Games 1991

    Nordic – Tourism, Canoeing

    Nordic – Tourism, Biking

    Aland Autonomy 70 years

    Church of Vardo

~

A Swedish squirrel summer snacking, 2007

ALAND'S FLAG

Six thousand five hundred fifty-four islands
Altogether amber glowing gateway
Russia ruled a century
(eighteen hundred nine to nineteen hundred seventeen)
Russian flag the Finnish flag
Russian revolution the Finnish revolution
Finnish revolution Aland return to Sweden squelched
   Alanders agitated
Autonomy Act Nineteen Hundred Twenty-Two
   Alanders agitated
Autonomy Act Nineteen Fifty-Two
   Alanders agitated
Autonomy Act Nineteen Ninety-three
   First flag blue yellow blue banned
   Sovereign Sundblom in nineteen thirty-five
   Decapitated Finnish flagpole to one foot above ground
   Finnish flag finished
   Nordic Cross divided into
     Swedish flag with a thin
       Bloodied cross inside the yellow
         Flying autonomously

~

A Swedish cat ready in a window, 2007

ALAND FRIMARKEN (STAMPS) III: 1992-1993

Aland's

- Cape Horn Congress
- Frans Peter von Knorring
- Lighthouses
- Joel Pettersson: Landscape
- Joel Pettersson: Self-portrait
- Aland's first Parliament
- Church of Hammarland
- New Autonomy Act
- Own postal administration
- Nordic – Fiddler
- Nordic – Boad shed
- Folk costume of Saltvik
- Folk costumes of Brando, Mariehamn and Eckero
- Folk costumes of Finstrom
- Diabase dyke
- Pillow lava
- Folded gneiss
- Church of Sottunga

~

American and Aland cousins meeting at the Port of Mariehamn, Aland, 2007

A Few Museums

Aland Art Museum in Mariehamn

The Aland Museum in Mariehamn

The Onningeby Museum, Onningeby

The Aland Hunting and Fishing Museum in Karingsund in Eckero

The Museum Ship Pommern in Mariehamn's West Harbour

The Aland Maritime Museum in Mariehamn

The Vita Bjorn Prison Museum in Kastelholm

Jan Karlsgarden in Kastelholm

Pellas Shipmater's House in Granboda in Lemland

The Labbas Homestead and Bank Museum, Storby, Eckero

Dano Homestead Museum in Geta

Kokar Homestead Museum on Hellso

Hermas Farm Museum on Enklinge in Kumlinge

The Museum of the Archipelago on Lappo in Brando

Akarpnato Farmstead Museum in Hammarland

The Aland Fire Brigade Museum, Morby in Hammarland

The Aland Museum of Photography, Kastelholm

The Museum of Owner's Marks in Ovanaker in Saltvik

~

Mariehamn Harbor, Aland Islands, 2007

BENGTS' *IRIS* *ECKERO

2011 becomes 1890
Sweden becomes Finland
Stockholm becomes Eckero
Iris becomes Aland

Precocious becomes unexploited
Dreams become potential
Death becomes life
Nature becomes romanticism

Vulnerability becomes its own reward
Process becomes the adventure
Little girls become women
Cinderella becomes the queen

Iris directed by Ulrika Bengts, a summer resident of the Aland Islands for 20 years, is the first feature film ever to be filmed on the Aland Islands and the first Finland-Swedish film for children.

~

Mini islands leading to Aland, 2007

ALAND ARTIST

Mortals do not trespass on his canvas.
There only themes
Emerge from the blazing blue
Aura of his abstracted eye, bestirring
The benevolent Baltic Sea blue ones.
Oil objects ooze
Through the hallucinating haze,
Representing reveries.
Pigmented implausible places penetrate the
Mask of the electro-magnetized mist.
The inanimate acts animate
With akvavit acumen.

Bohemians are brushed
By the fertility of his fanciful Finnish farm.
Even the mundane are moved
By the texture of his story-tale Teutonic tempest.
But the cast of his hallowed hand was colored
By Heaven.

~

*"The Flying Dutchman" oil on cardboard
by Arthur M. Carlson, 1916*

WORKING GIFTS

In the beginning
Before there were Carlsons, Danielsons, Mattsons,
And the like ~
Numerous nameless ancestors' daughters and sons
Made the Aland Sea hike
To become
Sailors, farmers, husbands, wives,
And for millennia
They would thrive
Continuing the line and the work
Some left, some stayed
Some bereft, some frayed
All the same on either side of the Atlantic ~
New millennia arrives and ancestral lives
Intersect and yet remain physically
Separated by an ocean ~
Now writers, ministers, counselors, artists,
Musicians, educators, administrators and thinkers,
Still husbands and wives
Still loving nature and the sea ~ Still.

~

Traveling by ship to the Aland Islands, 2007

FOLKVISA*

Tiptoeing trolls tread instead
Beneath the triplet rhythm
Of my braided hair over there
Where I cannot help but care
   Skipping turning dancing
   Turning dancing skipping;
Across the strings of bear sinew
And overbearing morning dew
Clothed in unspeakable birch tree air
With wood and wood wind to spare
   Laughing linking leaping
   Linking leaping laughing;
Struck by a howling wolf
Startled that I hear him
Signing me so far away
By willow flute from yesterday
   Fiddling drumming piping
   Drumming piping fiddling;
Crayons in the sky shiny kings
Choppy spit in rune root things
   Moose and herring hunters
   Reindeer and herring herders
   Potato and rutabaga wranglers
Sit in an empty closet off key off kilter

(Swedish: Folksong)

Isolated home on a granite island leading to the Aland Islands, 2007

UNPLAYED AT THE INSTITUTE OF MUSIC

This dusty damper is
Devoid of dynamic vibrations.
Snoozing strings drowse on
Undisturbed by hampered
Harmonizing hammers.
Sour spinster keys do not
Miss the sweet coupling
Touch of trilling fingers
On cool innocent ivory.
My magnificent mute mahogany,
Were I accomplished and you attuned
There would be no monotony for us.

~

UNPLAYED II
(sequel to "Unplayed")

Although I cannot make you
Sing with my faithless fingers,
I may press your delicate
Damper for a few resonant seconds,
Sing an ardent arpeggio into you
And cherish
The echo of striking a chord.

~

View of the Baltic from Eckero, Aland, 2007

TROLL TALE

A thousand trolls swam through the shoals
Chased all the way from Bergen
From Norway high to Sweden nigh
Hiding daily lurking

With all their kin they ventured in
The screaming frigid Baltic
Throughout the night with just star light
To guide them without faulting

Tiny to huge the troll deluge
Feared the sun at dawn
Scattering to flight left and right
Granite Aland Islands were spawned

~

Driving past fields on the roads of Eckero, Aland, 2007

DANCE OF THE TOMTE GNOME

A tomte gnome
Watches over our home
Mostly at night
But he stays out of sight ~
Even the cat
Doesn't glimpse his hat,
Pointy and red
After we go to bed
When he wanders
About, and he ponders,
No doubt, "Are they
All okay? Hooray!"
He takes a glance,
No one watching, he'll dance
Until the dawn
Stirs the sounds of small yawns ~
Away he goes,
Wiggling his big, round nose ~

~

Arriving from the Stockholm ferry to the Port of Mariehamn, Aland, 2007

THREE MAGICAL EVENTS THAT MIGRATED FROM SWEDEN

Number 1: for good luck in the coming year

> On New Year's Eve, eat an entire herring in one mouthful at midnight.

Number 2: to keep from drowning at sea

> Never sleep on your stomach.

Number 3: for success in moose hunting

> The night before a moose hunt, the hunting party must collectively make a drawing of the moose(s) they hope to catch. Then they must burn the drawing together, watching the flames consume it entirely.

~

Swedish flag flying from the Stockholm-Aland-Helskini ferry, 2007

ST. LUCIA'S DAY 2004, St. Petersburg
St. Petersburg, Florida

Wednesday, December 15, 2004 8:37 PM

Dear Diane,

On December 13, I prepared a St. Lucia's Day dinner as my turn to cook for the Monday evening Bible study "Seeking Wisdom" with the ladies of the Beautiful Hat Society of Pasadena Community Church.

As the ladies nibbled on *lingonberries* and Swedish meatballs, I related the story of St. Lucia, the 6th century Italian Christian martyr who centuries later became venerated by the Swedish people. Every year on December 13, Swedes worldwide celebrate St. Lucia's Day. Usually, the eldest daughter plays the role of St. Lucia, dressed in white with a crown wreath of candles (4 for Advent) and serves the family Lucia buns. However, if the family doesn't have a daughter, you make do...

At that very point in the story the doorbell rang. I opened the door. In came my husband dressed in full regalia, costume, wig, makeup as St. Lucia followed by my gay hairdresser friend carrying his train and a boom box blaring "Santa Lucia."

~

View of Aland countryside from the road, 2007

ALAND FRIMARKEN (STAMPS) IV: 1994-1995

Aland's
- Boulder field
- Drumlin
- Rundhall
- Butterflied (booklet)
- Europa – von Willebrand's disease
- Europa – Heparin
- Pottery
- Stone tools
- Settlement
- Church of Sund
- The Pitcher of Kallskar
- Erratic boulder
- Pothole
- Cargo Vessels of the archipelago (booklet)
- Europa – Peace and freedom (twice)
- Nordic – Sportfishing
- Nordic – Golf
- World Champ, Optimist Dingies
- The European Union
- St. Olaf
- Church of Geta

The Potato in Aland

Traces of sixteen Stone Age settlements
In the village of Langbergsoda
Beneath the Viking overland overlord
Harvest potatoes in Ovanaker
As far as their eyes cannot see
In West Saltvik the crisp factory in Haraldsby
Crisps, chips, frozen mash
Richer than Idaho, Irish
Ground granite Arctic soil
Tendrils of tuber till and toil
Magical manna manifestation
Organically
    I am growing my own
        In my own backyard
                For my own cultivation, consummation

Baking potatoes ready to be used in Swedish recipes
At Carlson smorgasbord, St. Petersburg, Florida, USA, 2010

BIG SALTVIK

ALAND'S BIGGEST
Municipality
Plain
Cave
Fields
Mountains
Beets
Potatoes
Viking market
Christian roots
View of the sea
Portal to the past

~

Wedding photo of Carl M. Carlson & Matilda Mattson

ST. LUCIA'S DAY 2008, Aland

Thursday, January 10, 2008

Dear Uncle Bob,

I just heard from our cousin Linda in Aland. It seems they had a splendid Christmas.

St. Lucia's Day began with Linda and the girls singing for Stefan while he was still in bed. She calls Mirah "the little one." Mirah was Lucia and Norah just wanted to be a small Santa or "tomte." It was really early because they were invited to Mirah's nursery school for a breakfast and Lucia festivities at seven in the morning. There Mirah was Lucia again with her friends, singing for all the teachers, parents and siblings. Some years, they go into Mariehamn proper to see Aland's "official" Lucia and her "girls" but this year they decided to stay at home.

Linda and her family celebrated Christmas at home with lots of friends and family visiting them. Christmas Eve they had dinner together with Stefan's dad and brother with family that live in Sweden, and Linda's dad. Her mom stayed at home since she had guests – her sister's family from Sweden. In the evening Santa arrived with presents. Early morning on Christmas Day Stefan was singing in the church choir while Linda and the girls slept in. The rest of Christmas consisted of coffee and dinner parties. They did more of the same on New Year's Eve.

Love,

~

Carlson family photo, Brooklyn, NY, early 1930s

From left: Ruth Johnson Carlson, Lloyd A. Carlson, Robert W. Carlson, Arthur M. Carlson

~

"To remember: We had five children, and three are still alive: Arthur, Carl, and Helen. Florence died of diphtheria at 5 years. Wilhelm died of some complaint after three months of life; he was a twin boy. Shall we gather at the river, the beautiful river, shall we gather with the saints at the river that flows by the throne of God."

Carl Mauritz Carlson

1869-1941

Aland and American Mattson cousins meeting at Port of Mariehamn, Aland, 2007

Von Willebrand's Disease

1926

Professor Erik Adolf von Willebrand

Discovered the disease named after him

Derivative of decreased factor eight

Deficient platelet function

Stagnant spontaneous stature

Profuse persistent prolonged

Pedigree in bleeder families

Parish endogamy until 1930s

Prone to nose bleeding and bruising

Fussing and fusing

A tall Aland gene

Smorgasbord of hemorrhagic disorders

Gangly kinship

Isolation

Imagine thirty indistinguishable
descendants from both sides

of the Atlantic milling about together
on the docks of the Port of Mariehamn

1988

My mother had von Willebrand's

From Aland, said the doctor.

My father's ancestry is from Aland, not my mother's.

Hers is German.

Aland Vikings made it to Germany, he said.

Transfusions   allusions   illusions

Coma

No coagulation

Sanguineous melting

Eyes, nose, ears and mouth seepage

Deluge the willowy sheets

Generational epochs of inbreeding

Oblivion leaking claret

~

Aland and American cousins gathering
at Mattson property, 2007

Digital Art by Jeannie Carlson, 2023
Genetic Anomalies in A land as a cell

GENETIC ANOMALIES IN ALAND

Baptismal Font at St. Lars Church, Eckero, Aland, 2007

ALAND FRIMARKEN (STAMPS) V: 1996-1997

Aland's

    Greeting bird

    Greeting fish

    Eagle Owl (booklet)

    Europa – Sally Alminen

    Europa – Fanny Sundstrom

    Song festival

    Karl Emanuel Jansson

    Fossils: Trilobit

    Fossils: Gastropode

    Church of Brando

    Spring flowers (booklet)

    Opossum shrimp and giant isopod

    Four-horned sculpin

    Ringed seal

    Women's World Floorball Championship

    Europa – Devil's Dance

    Kalmar Union 600 years

    Autonomy 75 years

    Steamship: S/S Thornbury

    Steamship: S/S Osmo

    Church of Mariehamn

~

Aland Apples

Catch the apples
Swimming in the orchards of Sund
Reeled in from the trees
To the hold of Tjudo
Vingard distilled
To the table enchanted
An apple in glass
Supplanted

Vastergards apple wine
Apple liqueur 'Appleaud'
Apple brandy 'Alvados'
Flavoured schnapps
Fermenting in time
Across the moat of Kastelholm

(Swedish: vineyard)

ST. LUCIA'S DAY 2008, Aland

St. Petersburg, Florida

Tuesday, December 09, 2008 11:26 AM

Dear Jenny,

Well, the *Sankta Lucia* solo went as well as it could go under the circumstances. The pianist from the Lutheran Church was in a fender-bender on his way over so he wasn't playing with all 88 keys. He arrived just as lunch started so he was over an hour late. We ran through one verse that went fine at that time. The room was full and there was applause for the rehearsal but by the time he'd eaten his salmon or prime rib, I think the impact of the crash was sinking in.

The piano hadn't been tuned in six years and there were serious problems with the microphone during the meeting portion of the get-together. When the microphone kept having issues, the Swedes starting calling out, "Get Obama – He can fix it!"

Dad ran off to see Phyllis about 15 minutes before I was about to sing. He couldn't wait. Even at 84...when a "stiffy" calls...

The club's treasurer read the story of Saint Lucia. Then I was up. The pianist started playing the intro before I got into position from the dinner table to the podium. I cleared three tables at full gallop in an attempt to make it to the front of the room and reach the podium in only two bars of intro... so I am frantically climbing over two people at the dais and getting tangled in the microphone wire that was worse than my computer cords. At least I stayed vertical.

By the time I got my music open and in position, I was already singing the first verse en route. I didn't do the repeat and went on to the second verse. The pianist couldn't figure out where I was in the music so he stopped playing. I kept going. He finally figured it out and chimed in. This time when we came to the repeat, I did the repeat and he didn't. Again, he stopped and I kept going. Verses one and two were in Swedish...you could say it got verse and verse. I did the third verse in Swedish and we somehow managed to stay somewhat together on that one. I sang the last verse in English – almost completely *a capella* (without accompaniment).

In true *UFF DA* fashion, I belted out the last verse and when I looked over at my husband, Tim, he had a huge smile on his face. By the way, through this whole debacle, ladies in Swedish folk costumes were distributing *pepparkakkor* (Swedish ginger snap cookies) – but no *glogg* (alcoholic spiced cider) this year, dammit. There was a general look of astonishment on everyone's face – except for Tim who was beaming.

The group's vice president came over to me afterward, complimenting my voice and presented me with a lovely pewter necklace charm of Sankta Lucia. The pianist played some Christmas carols for a sing-along after that and he didn't keep it together for the sing-along either. Not just anyone can "F"-up *Silent Night* – that's special. People came up to me and asked me what was wrong with him (I'd never met the man before that day). I just shrugged my shoulders and said that he had been in an accident on the way over. Tim couldn't stop smiling. He said, "This was the best Scandinavian Luncheon ever!"

God jul!

Picture the youngest descendant,
age 3 in horned Viking helmet and
full regalia.

*Timothy R. Burns dressed as St. Lucia for St. Lucia's Day
Celebration, 2013*

Kastelholm Castle

Nobles   feudal chiefs   kings
Kastelholm   castle   home
Rose a titan of Swedish monarchy
Thirteen eighty

Lord
    over the Baltic
    over the fjord to the south
    over grains
    over ship building
    over deposed king
    over a chapel
    over criminals
    over the post
    over mining
    over decay
Sentinel
    two gate towers
    eight Alanders in length
    walls two Alanders high
    brick and mortar strength
    withstanding   fire   cannon   passage   plowers

~

Carlson Vasa Bible, 2013

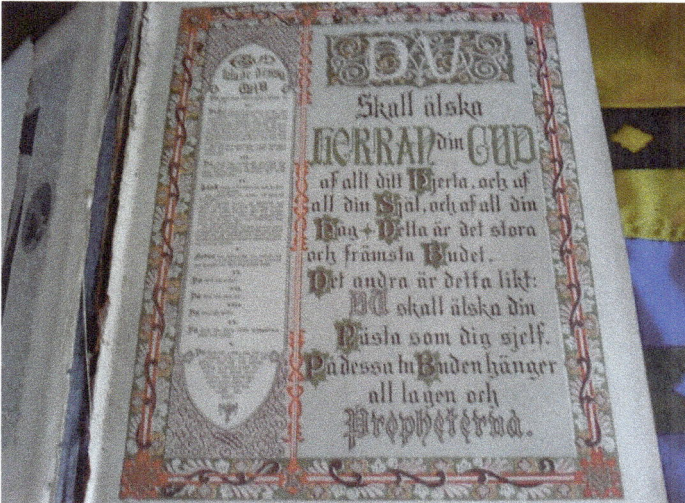

ALAND, CRADLE OF SCANDINAVIAN CHRISTIANITY

Jesus sailed to Saltvik* Salt Bay
Brackish waters bestowing on
Broad back of Bishop Ansgar* labor with ~
Midwives Unni and Hiltin to
Birca market town manger
Birthing in discretion
A safe distance from Uppsala*
With the blessing of Bjorn, Ragnar's son ~
New King Olaf's prayers for plunder
Answered in Archbishop Unni's rune
"I came to them" on the Borge* uncircumcised
Archeological indications of mission ~
Wooden predecessors to granite
Excavated by Carl O. Nordling*

(Saltvik: known today as Kvanbo)

(Ansgar appointed envoy to Sweden by Pope Gregorius IV: 827-44)
(Unni and Hiltin: assistants to Ansgar)

(Uppsala: center of Norse pagan temple)
(Bjorn: local ruler of Aland in Ansgar's time)

(Borge: a rocky hill near Saltvik with remains of an ancient stronghold)

(Twentieth century architect, urban planner, researcher, scholar, and expert in matters relating to Swedish-Finns)

"As a child I always looked at the pulpit built out from the wall, with a lot of carvings of a baby face and two gilded wings. The minister's uniform was white down to his heels with big sleeves and a cape across the back also down to his heels. There was a picture of Christ ascending, about 6 feet tall in the front of the altar."

Carl Mauritz Carlson

1869-1941

Altar of St. Lars Church, Eckero, Aland, 2007

St. Lars Church I

Aland red rapakivi granite
Thunder gemstone pedestal
Tarred shingle tower topping
Touched by a Roman martyr
Grilled in rock
A mere millennium before
Building Eckero's *kyrka*

Missing my family name
   commemorated in the church's
      contiguous cemetery
Twenty-four generations
Baptized   Married   Buried
There   there   there
Before the days of tombstones
Until the wooden crosses above
   their puny graves collapsed
Leaving
   the wildflowers
      as their markers

(Swedish: church)

Wild flowers and church grounds at St. Lars Church, Eckero, Aland, 2007

St. Lars Church II

Light floods the inside
Candled chandelier
Opposite a dangling replica of a tall ship
    Like a life preserver
    In the tiny church
    With the tiny blue pews
    Where the tiny crucifix hangs on the north wall
    On the tiny hill north
    Of the tiny Iron Age burial ground
Did great grandfather hear the early
Thirteenth century church bell not ring?

Christ carried all
    To Valhalla's higher ceiling
Where their souls
    Could stretch
    Tall

~

Graveyard at St. Lars Church, Eckero, Aland, 2007

GUSTAV VASA BIBLE AND THE SEAL MUSKET

Gold inlay, wood and iron
Humbling and fearsome both
Heirlooms of **Carl Mauritz Carlson**
To his eldest son **Arthur**, and then
To **Arthur**'s sons, **Lloyd** and **Bob**
Bible to **Lloyd**, sailor soldier skilled-engraver
Musket to **Bob**, pastor pacifist professor

Bible with iron locks
Musket without locks
Bible with illuminated manuscript
Musket with iron trigger
Bible with Swedish language
Musket without etymology
Bible with human ink and blood
Musket with seal's blood
Bible with potency
Musket without bullets
Bible with degeneration
Musket with rust

~

Carlson Vasa Bible, 2013

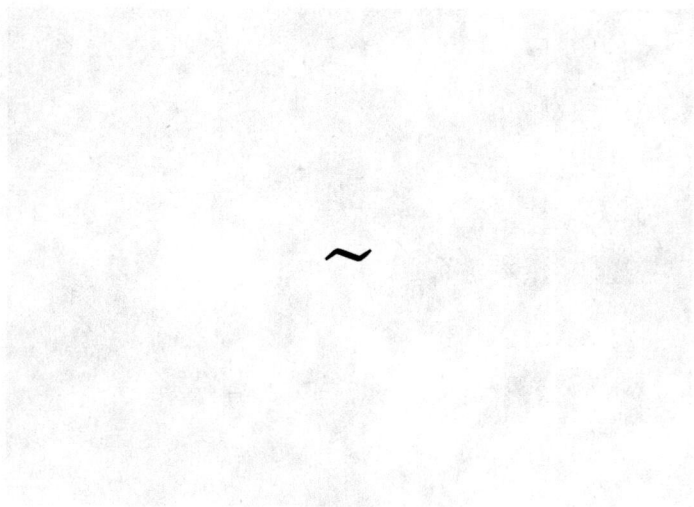

"In my grandfather's time, about 1808, there was a Russian-Swedish war, and Eckero was where they stopped their advance. There were all kinds of stories told to us children about the cruel Russians and how they stole everything they could put their hands on, especially cattle for food and they seemed to have their own way of locating hidden valuables. One story was that they dug below the barn where ships were kept. A story about their cruelty was the Russian sailors who tied a rope around an old man's legs and hitched it to a horse and made him gallop down the road for sport."

Carl Mauritz Carlson

1869-1941

Eddie Carlson holding the 1861 Danielson musket (seal gun), 2013

THE KUMLINGE BATTLE MEMORIAL 1809

Russian soldiers requiring rations
Armed Alandic agrarians refusing
Farmers mistaken for Swedish militia
Sharecropping fierce shots
Storing Russian prisoners
At Kumlinge parsonage
Oblivious to surrender flags
Aland's cultivators carried on
To win the battle
And lose the war
To win the chattel
And lose the core

Cenotaph constructed at Falberget
Floating off the coast of Sweden
Robert Liewendahl's theatrical composition
"Don't mess with Aland" cartoons at satwcomic.com

~

RUINS OF BOMARSUND FORTRESS

Crimean War
Summer 1854
Sund, Aland Islands, Baltic Sea
Anglo-French victory
>   Over Russian Empire
>   Overwhelming artillery fire

Treaty of Paris 1856
Demilitarized Aland Islands
Treaty stands
Ruins lie

During the Crimean War (1854-1856) over 300 conscripted "Finns" were captured at Bomarsund and imprisoned at Lewes in Sussex, England. The incarcerated officers (all Russian aristocrats) were housed as guests with local gentry while the "Finnish" soldiers were jailed in abhorrent conditions. Twenty years later Russia's Czar Alexander II commissioned a Russian Memorial to honor the 28 "Finnish" prisoners of war who perished in captivity. The memorial stands in the churchyard of St. John Sub Castro in Lewes. The 28 names are Swedish and Finnish, not Russian.

Digital Art by Jeannie Carlson, 2023

The 28 Names of the Finnish soldiers who died while incarcerated at Old County Gaol (Jail) as etched on the "Russian" Memorial at Lewes

28 NAMES

ALAND ISLANDS PEACE

Institute example of empowerment
Research robust results
Monitor Mariehamn's mutual respect
Survey the singularity of sea
Widowed of walloping waves
Evoking voluminous virulence
Calmed by crisis a century accord
Conclude conscription
Active perspective of peace
Bridging skerries
Armistice of neutrality and disarmament
Generosity of gender
Mobilization of minorities
Conserve culture
Obscure battlements
Still the struggle

CRYSTALLIZED:
A parody on Boris Pasternak

Drifting winter mountains
Pass my cold candlelight
Melting the frigid bed
Where my lover loved tonight.

I flicker on the crest
Of crystal window pane
Straining for reflections
Of Icy Eden again.

Granite along an Aland Islands inlet, 2007

ALAND FRIMARKEN (STAMPS) VI: 1998-1999

Aland's

    Horticulture: apples

    Horticulture: cucumbers

    Active youth (booklet)

    Europa – Midsummer celebration

    Nordic – Shipping

    International Year of the Ocean

    Sea scout camp

    Tennis (self-adhesive sheet)

    Seffers porch

    Labbas porch

    Abros porch

    Church of Eckero

    Bronze age: finds

    Bronze age: ship tumulus

    Folk art (booklet)

    Wheat trade 50 years

    Cowslip (self-adhesive sheet)

    Europa – Nature reserve

    Sailing

    UPU 125 years

~

CROSSED COAT OF ARMS

Nine blanched white Alandic roses
stationed Tic tac toe
all noughts no crosses unboxed
blazoned on a field of blue
holding two roe deer centrally stacked
pranced a province off to Oland, another island cluster
ample in deer but not in roses.
One heavily antlered gold red deer on a field of blue
gifted to Aland, meant for the other archipelago,
both recipients of the blunder.

Blessed *Riksheraldikerambet*!
Proofread the gaffe four centuries since
Gustav I lay sanctified in Swedish soil   ,
the roses disbursed in cemetery and sea,
Aland lost to the three crowns, foundering
amidst the latest world war of the roses.
The error?
rectified for Swedish Oland with a new grant
fortified for Finnish Aland with an old fury.

(1560 – Coats of Arms were designed for all Swedish provinces by order of King Gustav I)

(Swedish: *Swedish Herald of the Realm)*

(The coat of arms error was discovered in 1944 during WWII)

ANTHEM OF THE ALANDER

Alannigens sang all of us sang
Always the refrain twice again
Verse and verse
And verse and verse
About our straits
About our fates
None the worse

No one is an island
Or a thousand islands
No one is alone
In a skerry fisher village
In a scary sea
Speaking Swedish together
Free

Du gamla, Du fria
Of old and cold
Once song to the north
Severed and bold
Show us where we belong
Show us where we belong.

(Swedish: Song of the Alander)

(Swedish: Thou ancient, Thou free)

Digital Art by Jeannie Carlson, 2023
Aland cheese & castle stamps as keep

ALAND CHEESE & CASTLE STAMPS AS KEEP

Åland VÄRLDEN   *Åland* VÄRLDEN   *Åland* VÄRLDEN   *Åland* VÄRLDEN

Åland VÄRLDEN   *Åland* VÄRLDEN   *Åland* VÄRLDEN   *Åland* VÄRLDEN

Åland VÄRLDEN   *Åland* VÄRLDEN   *Åland* VÄRLDEN   *Åland* VÄRLDEN

~

"A number of girls had kids without being married. Some fathers had to pay to raise the child, and certain cases were settled by the court. If you intended to marry, you notified the minister and he advertised it from the pulpit four Sundays and then you would set the date."

Carl Mauritz Carlson

1869-1941

Aland inlet dock, 2007

ALANDIC SHIELDMAIDENS

Assertion of social identities
Now and then
Gender-neutrality now
Gender mythology then

Framework for thinking
Now and then
Erudite now
Instinctive then

Sexual freedom
Now and then
Multi-orgasms now
Orgasms then

Wealth and power
Now and then
More now
Some then

Value of voices
Now and then
Vernacular now
Skaldic verses then

~

Aland and American cousins lunching at Russell's Restaurant, Aland, 2007

FREYJA & ACTIVE ALAND VIKINGS

The Day of Freyja *Freyja's dag* Friday
a week before Freyja's day
July oozing into the first of her throne
Viking Market battling rye dancing tunics mead and mutton
spread over three days
a paste of her beauty fertility gold
crowning cycle of Scandinavia
ten thousand buckets of Vikings
swarm from fourteen countries
lineage in *Folkvangr*
assemble in Kvarnbo, Saltvik
reviving the embattled slain
vanquished vanity *Hus Vanir*
rattling the swords shields and sons of
Hlodver the Tall
twelve hundred years later

(Norse: afterlife field where Freyja receives half of those who die in battle)

(Norse: "house of Vanir," a group of gods known for their fertility, wisdom & ability to see into the future)

ULFBERHT SWORDS

Crucible steel slag free
exceeding medieval three thousand degrees
metallurgically a cut above
lacking brittle impurities
infinitesimal inclusions
enigma fashioned tightly two hundred years
sparring a millennium ago

tempered steel
welded letters in place
formed a blacksmith bishop's name
framed with fired crosses
quenched the hardening sword
with dragon's blood and oil

Secret steel
burnt bones hammered well in
empowering the blade
with the magic dust DNA
of wolves and ancestors
Spewing 171 from the old trade routes

Surstromming

Aland yards
See a small house
Like an outhouse
Smelling as bad
Fermented in salted brine
Barreled Baltic
Late spring herring
Ancient staple
Best adding
  onion, sour cream, chives, tomato, dill
  some, all or nil
Uncovered from a tin or museum
  in Skeppsmalen

(Swedish: Herring)

(north of the town of Oernskoeldsvik, Sweden)

Envision blonde Aland children playing in Brooklyn circa 1929.

Typical Swedish meal of herring prepared six ways, Vasa Museum, Stockholm, 2007

ALAND HOLIDAYS

Nineteen public holidays
Eleven Christian
Five pagan
Three political

Christian celebrations
All about Jesus
Pentecostal Epiphanal
Saints and sanctimonious

Heathen jamborees
Bonfires and students with white caps
Seasonal and solstice wingdings
No sacrifices

Patriotic commemorations
Peace after the Crimean
Freedom from Russia
Keeping the Swedish culture

~

Swedish Meatballs, boiled potatoes, and lingonberries, Vasa Museum, Stockholm, 2007

Midsommardagen

Heathen customs
Summer solstice celebration
St. John the Baptist adaptation
St. John's Wort picked
Magic concentrated
Maidens picked
    Seven kinds of flowers
Maidens jumped
    Seven fences
Maidens laid
    Seven flowers under their pillows
Maidens dreamed
    Seven ways to Sunday
Maidens sought
    Seven signs of besotting
        Aland mate

(Swedish: Mid-Summer's Day)

St. Lars Church and graveyard, Eckero, Aland, circa 1970

Photo taken by Rev. Robert W. Carlson

TRENDING OF RELIGION IN ALAND

Nothingness

Norse Paganism

Christianity

Lutheran Reformation

Evangelical Lutheranism

Secular Humanism

Liberalism

Nothingness

~

Interior of St. Lars Church, Eckero, Aland, 2007

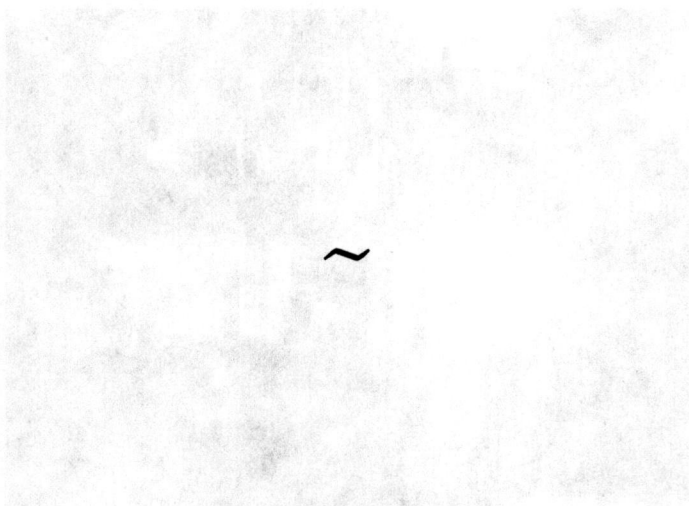

"One excitement on the island was when some sweetheart forgot to go home before the morning side of the night. If it was spring and already light; someone getting up early saw him running back home, sneaking around the back road, and there was scandal. Many stories like that were told – if it were not for my father and mother's prayers I probably would have been dragged in."

Carl Mauritz Carlson

1869 – 1941

COOPERATIVE CHEESE*

Cheese on a stamp

Cheese on a *Langsamofin*

Cheese on black Alandsbagarn* bread

Cheese on *hemvete**

Cheese on Mariehamn pizza

Cheese on

Cheese

Coat of arms on cheese packaging

Blue and yellow ribbon winners on best cheese

Kastelholm double on cream cheese

Quality savory on aroma cheese

Tiny mouse eyes mirrored on cheese

Medieval aged on sharp cheese

Skinny* on cheese

Kastelholm

Aland Special

Prostens magra

Edamost

Milk, Cream, Butter, Cheese

Most cheese

*Ost**

(Aland's Centralandelslag is the dairy cooperative founded in 1921)

(newer Alandic bread with a low GI index)

(Aland's bakery founded in 1951)

(Swedish: loaf sandwich)

(31% fat in Kastelholm cheese)

(These are the names of some of ACA's award-winning cheeses)

(Swedish: cheese)

Swedish Fontina, Danish Havarti and Scandic Farmers Cheeses
At Carlson Julborg, St. Petersburg, Florida, USA, 2015

MIDNIGHT SUN

Undulating snow clouds drift
Breathing deeply
And stroking
Incandescent cloudberry juice
Across its horizon
Lubricating the atmosphere
Melting the cold
With the fingers of the summer sun
Climaxing by the light
Of her own radiation

ALAND FRIMARKEN (STAMPS) VII: 2000-2009

Aland's
- Sea Birds: Artic tern
- Post Terminal
- Smooth Snake
- Great Crested Newt
- Mushrooms
- Predators: Ermine
- Predators: Red fox
- Predators: Pine marten
- Immigrated animal species: Greater cormorant
- Immigrated animal species: Whooper swan
- Immigrated animal species: Grey heron
- Beetles: Rose chafer
- Beetles: Seven-spot lady bug
- Beetles: Rhinoceros beetle
- Flowers: Sea asters
- Flowers: Purple loosestrife
- Flowers: Beach angelica
- Fishes: Perch
- Fishes: Zander
- Cows

"There was no protection from hunters. Ducks that came in the summer were almost wiped out. The most beautiful was called the IDER duck. Eckero people started to protect them even with no law."

Carl Mauritz Carlson

1869-1941

Danielson Seal Gun dated 1861

ALAND FRIMARKEN (STAMPS) VIII: 2010-2014

Aland's
- Passenger Ferries
- Scenery: coastline
- Scenery: mountains
- Christmas
- Peacock Butterfly
- Charity – Pink Ribbon
- Charity – Blue Ribbon
- Dragonflies
- Powerlifting
- My Aland – Robert Helenius
- Cat with a fishing rod
- Bellflower

~

~

"There were many stories passed down to us children, especially ghost stories, probably told to scare us so we wouldn't run out in the evenings. If you realize that there were no street lights, only black dark when you stepped out, it was easy to scare a child."

Carl Mauritz Carlson

1869-1941

ORIGINS

Two millennia back
Bones of the indigenous ancients
Long since melted into the granite

Eighty generations of Alanders
Ago landed

Forty-five family groups
Walked on frozen water
From Sweden's coast before it was Sweden

Pilgrims of the new covenant of Aland
When Christ walked on liquid water
At the same time

We descend from the forty-five
We ascend from the forty-five
We are Aland

~

Midnight sun over Mariehamn, Aland, 2007

~

ALAND A PROCESS ESSAY

When there is a mixing of the tangible and the intangible, poetry seems the most appropriate vehicle. One of my Aland cousins told me a few years back that Swedish is a dying language. From a third generation watchtower I observe the cultural light flickering. Ethnic traditions fold into the melting pot several generations post-immigration to America. A global society further assimilates the smaller nations into a diluted soup. The individuality disappears.

"...Sad how we do not remember that we were once giants."
-Steven Riley, 2012

Idiosyncratic

Suggestive not exhaustive

Meanderings

Aland A Land is fragmentary, puzzle-like with edges, a map where all roads lead to a source rather than a destination. Like Aland itself, interconnected islands dot the landscape to illustrate various contextualized vistas.

The height of a progenitor may be measured by the length the descendants are willing to traverse to locate particular strands of DNA.

Charles Olson's work initially inspired me but his vision is not my vision. I found myself more connected to Eleni Siklianos and Maggie Nelson on an emotional level but with snippets of Anne Waldman sneaking into my peripheral view. Add a condensory dab of Lorine Niedecker and a dusting of lists *a la* Georges Perec. These authors have some component of influence, infiltrating my process almost subconsciously like a subliminal suggestion. I perceive them lurking in the granite.

Akin to a new romantic relationship

Enchantment

Anxious for intercourse

Easily concerned for its existence

Jealous of what it knows and I don't

Worried about its future

Hungry and irrational

Pregnant with the investigation, the accumulation of information gestates. But then, there is not a single birth but multiple births, septuplets, seventy times seven. All of these offspring compose the familial unit, a cavalcade of creation that develops individually and collectively, a surprise. Manipulate, direct and cogitate these progeny but somehow, almost supernaturally, they evolve into their own. They may resemble me in aspect but somewhere along the line, they advance beyond the confines of the nature and nurture of their origination.

As I have learned in journalism, a precise quote is a vetted source even if it is a lie.

Landmark

proceeding from an ancestral source

a descendant seeks

 cursor

significance

consequence

configuration

Primary Sources

Aland, A Baltic Archipelago

Pastime – A Swede in America Looks Back: The Life Journal of Carl M. Carlson

A History of the Swedish People: Volumes 1 & 2

The essays of Carl O. Nordling

Swedish-English/English-Swedish Dictionaries

Aland Islands

Population Structures and Genetic Disorders: Seventh Sigrid Juselius Foundation

Secondary Sources

letters, emails, maps, sheet music, pictures, art, recipes, medical records, Google searches

Sensory Sources

Staring at the oil paintings my grandfather painted a century ago, *The Flying Dutchman* and *The Sea*

Gardening – adding Swedish coffee grounds to the soil

Singing Swedish hymns

Preparing and consuming Swedish food and drink

Lightly touching my family's Gustav Vasa Bible

Tripping to IKEA

Listening to Sibelius' *Finlandia*

Presiding over Suncoast Scandinavian Club meetings

Remembering changes nothing and everything. Understanding creates meaning. When a map is legible, there are choices in trajectory. The universe expands.

Overlapping Aland, mentally categorize segments, form

extending content. St. Lucia, meet St. Lars. Islands meet. Potatoes and apples meet. Cardamom and farina meet. Swedes and Finns meet. Alanders meet. Ships and sailors meet. Myth and hero meet. Castle and ruins meet. Flags and history meet. Midsummer and midwinter meet. Genetic disorders meet. Past and present meet. Meat and meat meet.

Facts as objects, observations are separate and distinct. Each tells its own story. When they are brought together, they tell a larger story. The truth is discerned from that.

The practical implications revolve around the senses, what I can perceive. These lead to historical, cultural and referential material. From there, the philosophical emerges.

Hybrid nature

   Exceed eulogizing

      Brilliant collage

         Multidimensional

            Scattered remnants

               –Jeannie Carlson

ABOUT THE AUTHOR

Jeannie Carlson is an award-winning writer experienced in fiction and non-fiction genres, with multiple freelance credits, published in newspapers, periodicals and books internationally. She has a bachelor's degree in theatre from Randolph-Macon Woman's College, Lynchburg, Virginia and a Master of Fine Arts in Creative Writing from Naropa University, Boulder, Colorado.

Born in the Scandinavian neighborhood of Bay Ridge in Brooklyn, New York, Jeannie grew up in the New York metropolitan area where she sang in professional theatre and opera. She is a NYC transplant, but considers herself a semi-native of St. Petersburg, Florida where she lives with her husband and their chatty housecat.

Jeannie is a correspondent for Tampa Bay Newspapers, Inc. as seen in Tampa Bay Times, TBNWeekly.com and Beach Beacon among others. She has taught English and English Literature courses at St. Petersburg College and Hillsborough Community College. A contributing writer for the Northeast Journal, Jeannie pens a bi-monthly poetry column, ONE Inspires where the results of her wandering the neighborhood come to fruition.

Visit her at www.JeannieCarlson.com.